The "Reason Why" Series

YOUR EYES

Irving and Ruth Adler

The John Day Company   New York

The "Reason Why" Series
by Irving and Ruth Adler

© 1962 by Irving and Ruth Adler

Library of Congress Catalogue Card Number: 62-16223

Contents

Your Eyes

Your eyes are wonderful things. They work for you all day long.

Your eyes help you learn about the world in which you live. They help you see things around you. They also help you learn about things you do not see when you read about them in books.

Your eyes help you learn many facts about the objects around you. Your eyes tell you if something is big or small. Your eyes tell you if something is near or far away. Your eyes tell you if something is solid or flat. Your eyes tell you about sizes and shapes and distances. Your eyes also tell you the colors of things and if they are bumpy or smooth.

Your eyes and hands work together as a team. Your eyes guide you when you do things with your hands. Then you can use tools for making things and toys and games for playing. You can hold a book and read it.

In this book you will find out how your eyes do all this work for you. You will find out how eyes may get out of order and how they can be fixed. You will find out about people whose eyes never can be fixed. You will find out how your eyes sometimes fool you. And you will find out what you must do to keep your eyes healthy so that they can keep working for you all your life.

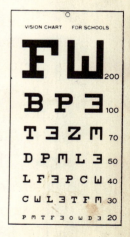

VISION CHART   FOR SCHOOLS

F W 200
B P E 100
T E Z M 70
D P M L E 50
L F E P C W 40
C W L E T F M 30
P M T F E O W D E 20

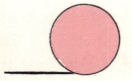

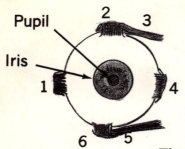

Pupil

Iris

1, 2, 3, 4, 5 and 6 are the muscles that join the eyeball to the socket

The eye from the outside

Partners in Seeing

There are three parts of your body that work together to make you see. The eye, the *optic nerve* (OP-tick) and the *brain* work together like three partners. The optic nerve and the brain are inside the head, so they cannot be seen.

The eye looks like a small white ball. It is set in a cup-shaped space in the front of the head. It is set in the eye *socket* (SOCK-et). Little muscles join the eyeball to the socket. They make the eyeball move. Folds of skin called the *eyelid* come down over the eye and hide part of it. The eyeball is about 1 inch across.

The first picture shows what the eye looks like from the outside. The picture is just about the same size as your eye. The colored part of the eye is called the *iris* (EYE-riss). The black dot in the center of the iris is an opening that lets light into the eye. It is called the *pupil*.

The second picture shows what the eye would look like if half of it were cut away.

The cornea (CORE-nee-a) is like a clear, glass window. It lets light into the eye. It keeps everything else out of the eye. It protects the inside of the eye.

The *lens* is like clear glass also. It has a light yellow color. The lens is held in place by little muscles. The muscles can change the shape of the lens.

The *retina* (RET-in-a) lines the inside of the eyeball. The part of the retina right in back of the lens is called the *fovea* (FO-vee-a). It is a yellow dot as big as a pin-head.

There is a dark layer between the retina and the hard white outside of the eye. This layer is like a window shade. It keeps light out. So light can come into the eye only through the pupil. The iris is part of this dark layer.

The optic nerve connects the eye with the brain.

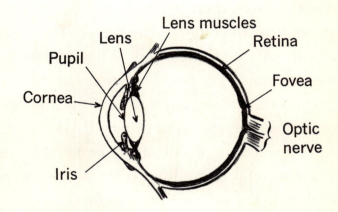

The eye with half of it cut away

The Retina

Rods

The smallest part of your body is a *cell* (SELL). There are muscle cells and bone cells. There are skin cells and blood cells. Each kind of cell does its own special kind of work.

The *rods* and *cones* are the special cells of the retina. They do their work when light shines on them. The rods do their work in dim light. The cones are used in bright light. They are also used for seeing colors.

The fovea, the spot on the retina right behind the lens, has only cones. So this is the part of the retina that sees best in bright light. This is the part of the retina that sees color well. When you look straight at something, light from it falls on the fovea. So if you want to see something clearly, you look straight at it.

Cones

Outside the fovea there are rods and cones. But there are no cones near the edge of the retina. There are only rods that can see dim things well. When you look out of the corner of your eye, you are using the edge of the retina. So you cannot see any colors out of the corner of your eye. But you can see dim things. If you want to see a dim star, you look at it out of the corner of your eye. When it is dark you use only rods for seeing. So you do not see colors in the evening or at night.

There is a part of the retina that has no rods or cones. The retina has no rods or cones where it joins the optic nerve. So this part of your eye is blind. This *blind spot* is near the fovea. Each eye has a blind spot.

The picture on this page will help you find the blind spot in your eye. Hold the book as far from you as you can. Cover your left eye and look straight at the X with your right eye. You will see the dot out of the corner of your eye. Then slowly move the book toward you. Be sure that you keep looking straight at the X all the time. Suddenly you will stop seeing the dot out of the corner of your eye. Keep moving the book toward you. You will start seeing the dot again.

You stopped seeing the dot when light from it fell on the part of the retina that had no rods or cones. Then light from the dot fell on the blind spot which cannot see anything.

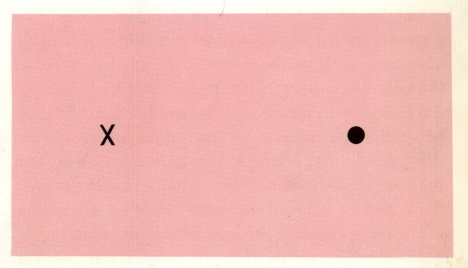

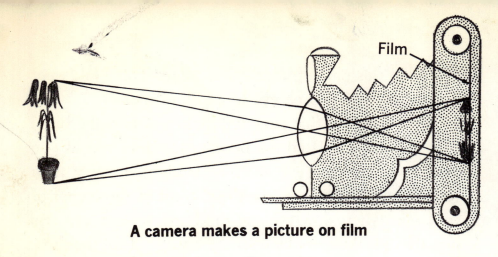

Film

A camera makes a picture on film

A Natural Camera

Your eye works the way a camera does. A camera makes a picture on the film you put into it. Your eye makes a picture on the retina.

Here is the way your eye makes a picture on the retina.

Light travels in straight lines called *rays*. When you look at something, rays of light from it reach your eyes.

The light first travels through the clear cornea. The cornea is not flat like a window. It is *curved* like a ball. The curved cornea bends the light so that it passes through the opening in the iris, the pupil.

The lens, which is behind the pupil, is curved too. It bends the light some more and forms a clear, upside-down picture of the thing you are looking at. We say that the lens *focuses* (FOE-cuss-es) the light. The clear upside-down picture is called an *image* (IMM-ij). For people who have good eyes, the lens focuses the light on the retina. Then there is a clear image on the retina. The

10

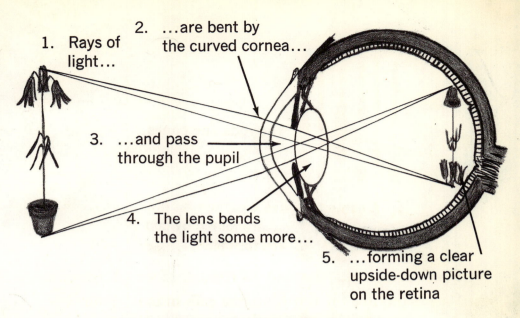

1. Rays of light...

2. ...are bent by the curved cornea...

3. ...and pass through the pupil

4. The lens bends the light some more...

5. ...forming a clear upside-down picture on the retina

Your eye makes a picture on the retina

lens does not focus blue light as well as light of other colors. The yellow color of the lens and the fovea keep a lot of blue light out of the eye. This is why the image on the retina of colored things is still sharp and clear.

The little muscles that hold the lens in place also change the shape of the lens. They make the lens thinner when you look at something far away. The thin lens focuses a clear image of the faraway object on the retina. The muscles make the lens thicker when you look at something nearby. Then the thick lens focuses a clear image of the nearby object on the retina.

So people who have good eyes always see things clearly.

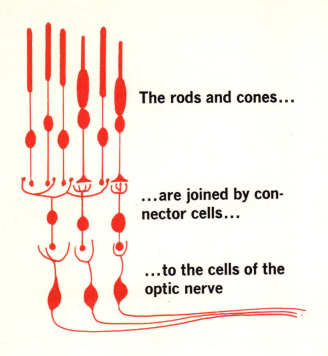

The rods and cones...

...are joined by connector cells...

...to the cells of the optic nerve

How the Seeing Partnership Works

There are millions of rods and cones in the retina. There are millions of connector cells in the retina, too. The connector cells connect with the rods and cones. They also connect with cells in the retina that look like fine threads. The fine threads come together at the blind spot to make the optic nerve. So the optic nerve is a bundle of threads. The optic nerve goes to the brain. There are two optic nerves, one for each eye.

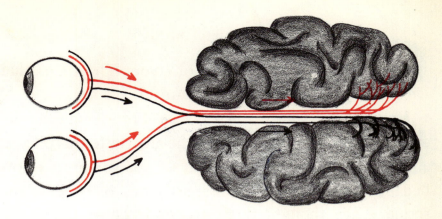

Each half of the brain is connected with both eyes

On the way to the brain, the two optic nerves come together. They cross over each other and separate again. When they cross over each other, the threads from the two optic nerves get mixed up. When they separate again, each optic nerve has threads from *both* eyes.

The brain looks something like the meat of a walnut. It has many folds. It has two halves. The back part of the brain has to do with seeing. An optic nerve ends in each half at the back of the brain. So each half of the brain is connected with both eyes.

When light shines on the retina, the rods and cones get to work. They get to work by making tiny electric currents. The optic nerves carry the electric currents to the brain. The brain puts together the meaning of these electric currents. It puts the meaning together as the *picture* that you *see*.

13

The Colors You See

The world around us is full of colors. The colors that we see help make the world beautiful.

How we see color is still a puzzle. For a long time scientists have been trying to find the answer to this puzzle.

Scientists used to think that we see different colors because there are three different kinds of cone in the retina. They thought there are some cones that work only when red light shines on them. They thought there are other cones that work only when blue light shines on them. And they thought there are still other cones that work when only green light shines on them. They thought that you can see other colors when some of the cones work together. For example, they thought you see yellow when the "red" and "green" cones work together and send messages to the brain. There is one thing wrong with this explanation. No one has shown that there are three different kinds of cone.

Edwin Land, the inventor of the Polaroid Land camera, did an experiment that makes him think we see colors in a different way. He took two black and white pictures of the same colored things at the same time. The two black and white pictures didn't look exactly alike. He kept all light except red light out of the camera when he made the first picture. He kept all light except blue light out of the camera when he made the second picture.

When these cones work together

You see

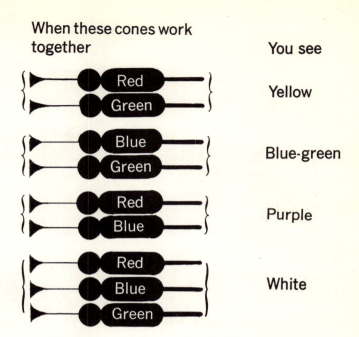

		You see
Red / Green		Yellow
Blue / Green		Blue-green
Red / Blue		Purple
Red / Blue / Green		White

The old idea about how we see color

He then flashed the first picture onto a screen, using red light. He flashed the second picture onto the same screen using blue light. The pictures on the screen were exactly on top of each other, making one picture. The picture he saw on the screen had all the colors of the things he had taken pictures of.

Land thinks we see different colors when different parts of the eye get different amounts of red and blue light.

Scientists will have to study this problem some more before they really understand exactly how the eye sees color.

15

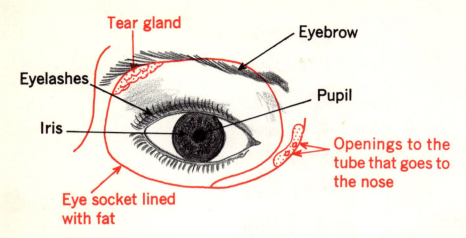

Tear gland

Eyebrow

Eyelashes

Pupil

Iris

Openings to the
tube that goes to
the nose

Eye socket lined
with fat

The parts in red are inside the head, so you cannot see them

The eye's protectors

Built-in Protectors

The eye can be hurt by hard blows. It can be hurt by flying bits of dust and metal. It can be hurt by too much light. But the eye is hardly ever hurt. It is hardly ever hurt because parts of the head and face protect it.

The eye socket is a bony cup. The hard bone of the head helps protect the eye from blows. The socket is lined with fat. So the eye rests on a soft cushion.

The eyelids close very quickly or *wink* when anything comes near the eye. They wink all by themselves. By winking they keep moving things from hitting the eyes.

The eyelids wink even when there is nothing near the

eye. They wink all day long. They keep winking, because the cornea must be kept wet. There are glands near the eyes that make tears. Winking spreads tears over the cornea. This is why it is hard to stare for a long time. When you stare, the cornea gets dry. Then the eyelids wink to make the cornea wet. Usually the tear glands make just enough tears to keep the cornea wet. When you cry they make a lot of tears. Then the tears spill out and run down your face. They also go down a little tube into your nose. That is why you have to blow your nose when you cry.

The iris has little muscles in it. These muscles can make the pupil bigger or smaller. When you look at something very bright, a lot of light reaches the eye. When a lot of light reaches the eye, the pupil becomes small. The small pupil does not let too much light into the eye. Too much light could hurt the retina. When you look at something dark, very little light reaches the eye. Then the pupil gets very big. The big pupil lets enough light into the eye so that you can see the dark object. The iris makes the pupil bigger and smaller all by itself.

Eyelids and eyelashes also help to keep things out of the eyes.

Eyebrows shade the eyes from the sun. They also work like the rain gutter on a house, catching the rain and making it run off the sides of your face instead of into your eyes.

Finding Out About Distances and Shapes

You can find out if things are nearby or far away without measuring. You can find out if things are flat or solid without feeling them. You can find out about *distances* and *shapes* by what you see.

Watch a car coming down the road. You can tell how far away the car is by how small it looks to you. When the car is very far away it looks like a dot. As the car comes nearer, it seems to get bigger and bigger. How big the car seems to be tells you about its distance. So, how big something *looks* helps you find out about distance. In the picture there are three blocks that are just the same size. The block that *looks* the biggest is nearest. The block that *looks* smallest is farthest away.

If you ride in a car, you will see another way of finding out about distance. As the car moves along, watch the trees that you pass. They all look as though they are moving the other way. The trees that are near the road

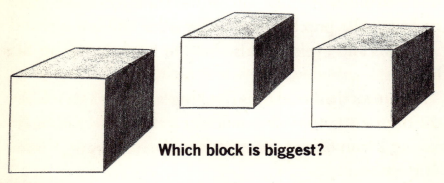

Which block is biggest?

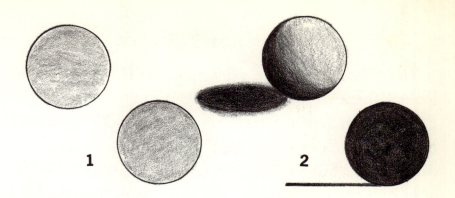

1   2

seem to move past you very quickly. Soon they are out of sight. The trees that are far away do not seem to move so fast. You keep seeing them for quite a while. So, how fast something *seems to move past you* helps you find out about distance.

In the first picture on this page you see two objects that look alike. They both have the shape of circles. They look alike because the light is shining straight on them, so you can see no shadows. In the second picture you see the same things when the light shines on them from one side. Now there are shadows that you can see. The shadows show you that one of the objects is a solid ball and the other is a flat circle. The solid ball has a round shadow. There are shadows on the ball, too. The flat circle has a shadow that is a straight line. There are no shadows on the flat circle. The shadows help you tell the difference between the solid ball and the flat circle. So you can learn about the shapes of things by the shapes of their shadows.

You also find out about the shapes of things when you look at them with two eyes.

When you look at something with two eyes, light from it reaches each eye. An image of the object is made on each retina. But you do not see two pictures. You see only one picture because the brain puts together the messages from the two eyes into a single picture.

The picture you see with two eyes is not like the picture you take with a plain camera. In a camera picture it is hard to tell things that are solid from things that are flat. The picture you see with two eyes makes it easy to find out the things that are solid and the things that are flat. Here is why.

The picture you see with two eyes is made up of the picture you see with the left eye and the picture you see with the right eye. These two pictures are a little bit different.

You can prove that each eye sees a different picture by holding up a pencil and looking at it. First look at it with your left eye. Then look at the pencil with your right eye. You will see more of the left side of the pencil with your left eye. You will see more of the right side of the pencil with your right eye.

Now look at the pencil with both eyes. You will see

20

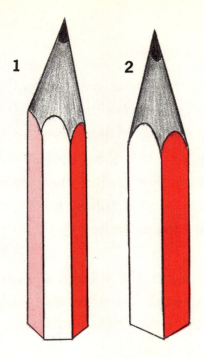

1. Left-eye picture. You see more of the left side

2. Right-eye picture. You see more of the right side

the left-eye picture and the right-eye picture at the same time. This makes the pencil look solid.

Plain camera pictures that you look at in a *stereoscope* (STEER-ee-o-scope) look solid, too. This is because the pictures are taken in a special way. A stereoscope uses two pictures of the same thing. The pictures are made by two cameras that are placed side by side like two eyes. So one picture is a left-camera picture. The other picture is a right-camera picture. When you look into a stereoscope, both pictures come together and make one picture. This makes the picture look solid. This is how 3-D movies are made.

21

Learning to See

When healthy babies are born, their eyes have all the partners they need for seeing. But newborn babies do not see the way you do. They have to learn how to see.

In the beginning, babies can tell the difference between bright things and dark things. But they cannot see shapes clearly. Their eyes cannot follow things that move. So they really cannot *look at* things the way you can.

By the time a baby is two weeks old, it begins to really look at things. Its two eyes work together and follow things that move in front of them. It can see shapes more clearly. It looks at faces closely.

Babies cannot see colors until they are two or three months old. Until then, they cannot tell the difference between colors and gray.

As a baby grows older, it learns to look at things for a longer time. It learns to pay attention to the things that it sees.

When a baby pays attention to the things that it sees, it learns more about its new world. It starts to use other parts of its body to help its eyes learn. At first, as a baby looks at things, it opens and shuts its hands. But it does not reach for the things it sees. As a baby gets older, it learns how to make its hands and eyes work together. Its

22

hands learn how to follow messages that are sent to its brain by its eyes. So, when a baby is five months old, it reaches for things that are held in front of it. It grasps things that it sees. The baby looks at the things that it grasps. With its hands and eyes working together, it learns more about the world.

Eyes and hands working together

Seeing in the Dark

When you go out into the dark night you can hardly see anything at first. Then the pupils of your eyes get larger. The light that comes into your eyes is dim. So you stop seeing with the cones of the retina. You begin to see with the rods.

But the rods do not get to work right away. It takes time for them to get used to the dark. As the rods get used to the dark, you can see more and more. You can make out the shapes of things even on a very dark night. You can walk along a road without a flashlight even on a very dark night.

The rods of some people take a very long time getting used to the dark. These people may not be able to make out shapes in the dark for many hours. These people are *night-blind*. They must be very careful when they go out into the dark. They may fall and hurt themselves.

Some night-blind people can begin to see better at night by taking a lot of vitamin A. Some night-blind people pass their night blindness on to their children.

Even people who are not night-blind can be helped to see better when they go from a place where there is a lot of light to a place where there is not much light. They can be helped to see better if they do not change quickly from seeing bright things to seeing dark things.

People who drive cars at night turn on their dim lights when another car comes toward them

Auto tunnels have brighter lights near the end than in the middle. Then the change from bright daylight to dim light is made more slowly.

Airplane pilots who fly at night wear dark glasses during the daytime. The dark glasses make the eyes use rods for seeing even in the daytime. Then the rods are used to the dark for seeing at night.

People who drive cars at night turn on their dim lights when another car comes toward them. Then their lights do not make the other driver night-blind. They keep lights off inside their cars, too. Then they do not become night-blind themselves.

What Are Good Eyes?

We need to see clearly in order to do most things. We need to see printed letters clearly in order to learn to read well. We need to see road signs clearly in order to drive safely. The dressmaker, the watchmaker and the machinist must all see clearly to do their work.

We can find out whether we see clearly by having our eyes tested. School children have their eyes tested each year. Automobile drivers have their eyes tested when they take a driving test. Many workers have their eyes tested when they get their jobs.

The picture on the next page shows a *Snellen* chart. The Snellen chart is used for testing eyes. The letters on a real test chart are 4 times as big as the letters in this picture.

You stand 20 feet from the chart when your eyes are being tested. You read the letters on the chart, first with one eye and then with the other. So each eye is tested separately.

If the smallest letters that you see clearly are in the eighth line, you have *normal vision*. This is the line that most people can see clearly when they stand 20 feet away from the chart. People with normal vision have 20/20 vision. It means that they can see at 20 feet what most people see at 20 feet.

If the smallest letters that you see clearly are in the

E

200

Y L V

120

U F V P

80

N R T S F

60

O C L G T R

50

U P N E S R H

40

T O R E C H B P

30

T V H P R U C F N C 20

third line, then you have 20/80 vision. It means that you have to be 20 feet from the chart to see what most people can see at 80 feet.

If you can only see the top line clearly, you have 20/200 vision. It means that you have to be 20 feet from the chart to see what most people see at 200 feet.

You can use the chart in this book for testing your eyes. But you must stand 5 feet away from this chart, because the letters are one-fourth as big as on a regular test chart.

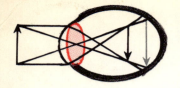
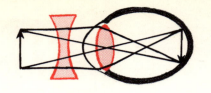

1. The clear image is in front of the retina. So the image on the retina is blurred

2. The concave lens puts the clear image on the retina

Eyes That Are Out of Order

Many people do not have normal vision.

Some people do not have normal vision because the eyeball is not the right shape.

If the eyeball is too long, the eye may be *nearsighted*. No matter how hard the little lens muscles work, they cannot make the lens focus on the retina. The clear image is made in front of the retina. So the image on the retina is blurred. The first picture shows how a nearsighted eye sees something. Nearsighted people can see clearly if they wear eyeglasses. The lenses of the eyeglasses help the lenses of the eyes do their work. Nearsighted people wear eyeglasses with *concave* (KON-cave) lenses. Lenses like this are thinner in the middle than they are at the edge. The second picture shows you how a concave lens makes a nearsighted person see clearly.

If the eyeball is too short, the eye may be *farsighted*. The lens of the eye makes a clear image in back of the retina. So the image on the retina is blurred. People who are farsighted wear eyeglasses with *convex* (KON-vex)

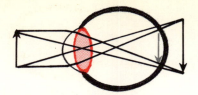

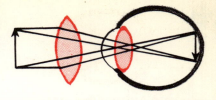

3. The clear image is in back of the retina. So the image on the retina is blurred

4. The convex lens puts the clear image on the retina

lenses. Lenses like this are thicker in the middle than they are at the edge. The pictures show you how a convex lens helps a farsighted person.

As people get older, the lenses of their eyes get stiffer. The little muscles cannot make the lens thicker for seeing things nearby. So the lens cannot make a clear image on the retina. This is a kind of farsightedness that is called *old sight*. Many people start having old sight when they are forty or forty-five years old. Old sight can be corrected by wearing eyeglasses with convex lenses.

There are people who do not see clearly because their lenses or corneas do not have the right shape. Their lenses cannot form a clear image of the things they see. These people have *astigmatism* (a-STIG-ma-tism). They can see better with eyeglass lenses that curve like the side of a drinking glass.

Sometimes people do not see clearly because the muscles that move the eyes do not work together. These people can usually be helped by wearing eyeglasses. Sometimes operations on the muscles are done.

In the United States about one person out of every five wears eyeglasses.

People Who Cannot See

People who cannot see are *blind*. Some blind people cannot see anything at all. Some blind people can see shapes and bright and dim lights. But they cannot see anything clearly, even with the help of eyeglasses. People are considered blind if their vision is no better than 20/200, even with the help of eyeglasses. There are about 14 million blind people in the world today.

Some people are blind because they are born that way. Other people become blind. Some people become blind from sickness or from not having enough food to eat. Some people become blind when an eye is hurt. Some people become blind when the optic nerve or the seeing part of the brain is damaged. Some people become blind when the cornea or lens gets clouded over and does not let light enter the eye.

People who cannot see can learn how to do many things.

People who cannot see can learn how to read. They read by using their fingertips. Instead of the ordinary alphabet that seeing people use, blind people use a *Braille* (BRAIL) alphabet. In the Braille alphabet, each letter is a pattern of bumps made in the paper. The blind person learns the patterns of all the letters of the alphabet. By feeling the bumps, he can spell out words. There are tools that a blind person can use to write Braille, too.

A blind person reading a Braille book

There are Braille libraries for blind people. There are *Talking Book* libraries for blind people, too. Talking Book libraries have phonograph records and tape recordings of books.

Blind people can be taught to lead useful lives. They can work at many jobs. They can become farmers, office workers and factory workers. Blind people can even go to college and learn professions. There are blind teachers, lawyers, ministers and doctors. Blind people who are trained do their jobs as well as people who can see.

New Eyes for the Blind

Some people become blind when the cornea gets cloudy. Then the cornea doesn't look like clear glass any longer. It looks like a milky glass. It does not let light into the eye.

These blind people can be made to see again. They can be made to see by an operation. In the operation, a little square window is cut in the cornea. Then a little bit of clear healthy cornea is fitted into the little window and sewn in place. Now light can get into the eye through the little square of clear cornea. The blind person can see again. In some operations all of the cloudy cornea is cut out. A whole healthy cornea is put in its place.

Healthy corneas for blind people come from an *eye bank*. Many people with good eyes give their eyes to an eye bank when they die. Then their healthy eyes can give happiness to a blind person by making him see again.

Some people become blind when their lenses get cloudy. The cloudy lenses do not let light into the eye.

An operation can make these blind people see again, too. In the operation, the cloudy lenses are taken out. These people must be fitted with special eyeglasses to take the place of the cloudy lenses. The eyeglasses have very thick lenses. With these eyeglasses, they can see almost as well as when they had their own, healthy lenses.

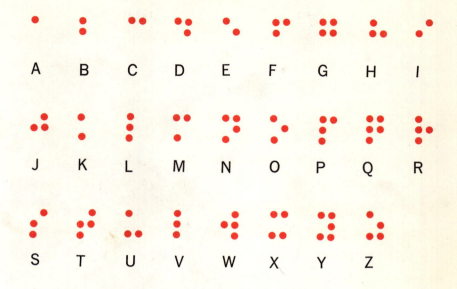

The Braille alphabet

Schools for Children Who Are Almost Blind

In many places children who are almost blind go to the same schools as children who have normal vision. They are happier when they go to the regular schools.

These children have special classes where they are taught to read and write Braille. They also read from special books that are printed in type as large as **THIS**. They have all their other classes with children who see well. Care is taken in choosing their teachers, however. Teachers who are kind and who write very large and clearly are chosen for them.

A Dog That Sees for Its Master

There are dogs that serve as eyes for blind people. They help blind people walk along crowded city streets. They help blind people walk through busy places like stores and railroad stations, factories and schools. These dogs are *Seeing Eye* dogs.

Seeing Eye dogs and the blind people whom they help are trained at a special school called The Seeing Eye. The dogs are trained to avoid danger. They are trained to follow commands. They are trained to obey words like "forward," "right," or "left." The Seeing Eye dog wears a special harness. In this harness, the dog leads the blind person safely as it follows his commands. German shepherd dogs and boxers are among the dogs used as Seeing Eyes.

Before a dog is given to a blind person, it is trained by a teacher who can see. It takes three months to train a Seeing Eye dog. After the training period, the dog is given a test. The teacher makes believe he is blind by covering his eyes with a black mask. He tests the dog by having the dog lead him across busy city streets. When the dog has passed the test, it is ready to lead a blind person.

A blind person lives at the school while he learns how to handle his dog and how to care for it. The blind person's training takes about one month.

Blind people do not like to be pitied. They want to be treated like everyone else. For this reason, The Seeing Eye expects the blind whom they help to pay for their dogs. It expects them to pay for their room and board at the school, too. They pay only $150 for all of this. If a person cannot pay, then the school helps him.

When a Seeing Eye dog gets old and dies, its blind master may come back to the school for another dog. He has to be trained again to use his new dog. This time he pays only $50.

The Seeing Eye is thirty-three years old. It has given dogs to more than 2,700 people.

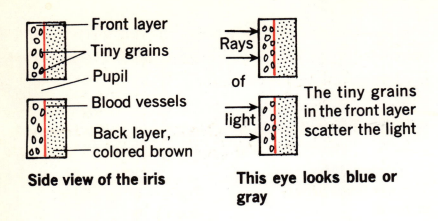

Side view of the iris

This eye looks blue or gray

The Color of Your Eyes

People have blue eyes, gray eyes, brown eyes or hazel eyes. A few people even have pink eyes. No matter what color eyes are, the color is made by the iris.

The iris has two layers. The front layer has many tiny grains in it. It also has blood vessels. Sometimes the iris has bits of brown or yellow coloring between the tiny grains. The back layer of the iris is colored dark brown.

When the front layer of the iris has no brown or yellow coloring in it the eye looks blue or gray. This is because the little grains in the front layer scatter light that shines on the iris. The scattered light looks blue.

When the front layer of the iris has brown or yellow coloring in it, the light is not scattered by the little grains. So you see the brown or yellow coloring. Eyes with brown coloring look brown. Eyes with yellow coloring look hazel.

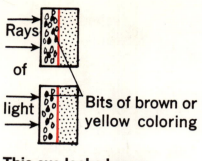

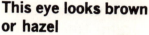
Bits of brown or yellow coloring

This eye looks brown or hazel

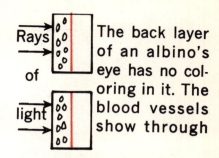
The back layer of an albino's eye has no coloring in it. The blood vessels show through

The eye of an albino looks pink

Sometimes the back layer of the iris has no coloring in it. There is no coloring in the front layer either. Then the red color of the blood vessels can be seen. Such eyes look pink. People who have no coloring in their eyes have no coloring in their hair or skin, either. They are called *albinos* (al-BY-nos). The dark coloring at the back of the iris helps keep light out of the eyes. But albinos do not have this dark coloring. So their eyes are hurt easily by bright light. They keep their eyelids partly closed to keep bright light out of their eyes. Albinos often have weak eyes. People who are albinos are born that way.

Eye color is something else people are born with. They *inherit* (in-HERR-it) it from their parents. Blue-eyed parents can have only blue-eyed children. Brown-eyed parents can have children with brown eyes or children with blue eyes.

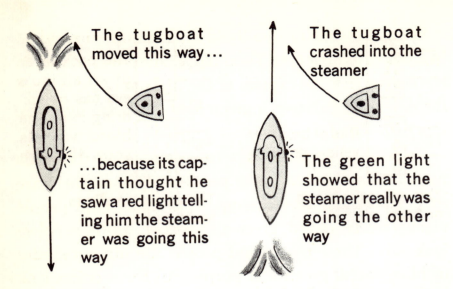

The tugboat moved this way...

...because its captain thought he saw a red light telling him the steamer was going this way

The tugboat crashed into the steamer

The green light showed that the steamer really was going the other way

Colors Some People Don't See

One clear summer night in 1875, a tugboat crashed into a steamer in the harbor of Norfolk, Virginia. Ten people were killed.

The officers of the steamer blamed the tugboat. They said the tugboat could surely see the green lights on the right side of the ship. They said the green lights told the tugboat that the steamer was moving toward the tugboat's right.

The tugboat captain blamed the steamer. He said he saw the red lights on the left side of the steamer. The red lights told him that the steamer was moving toward the tugboat's left. So the tugboat captain steered his tugboat toward the right. He crashed into the steamer, because the steamer really was moving toward his right.

For a long time no one could explain how an accident like this could happen. Then the mystery was solved. It turned out that the captain of the tugboat could not tell the difference between a green light and a red light! He was *color-blind*.

Color-blind people usually can see colors. But they do not see colors the way most people see them. There are some colors that they mix up. Most color-blind people mix up shades of red, green and yellow. All these colors look alike. These color-blind people also mix up shades of blue, bluish green and purple. All these colors look alike to them. But these color-blind people never mix up red, green or yellow with blue or purple. They can easily tell these colors apart.

There are a few color-blind people who can see no color at all. To people who see no color at all the world looks like a big black and white picture.

People who are color-blind can cause accidents. The locomotive engineer must be able to tell the difference between a red light and a green light. So must the airplane pilot and people who drive cars. Locomotive engineers and airplane pilots are tested to find out if they are color-blind. In some places, people who drive cars are tested for color blindness, too.

About one in every four persons is color-blind. Color blindness is usually inherited. There are more color-blind men than women.

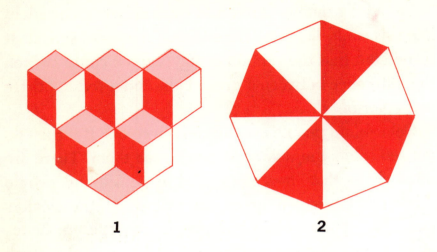

1   **2**

Some Strange Things Your Eyes Do

Look carefully at the pictures on this page.

The first picture shows some blocks. Can you tell how many blocks there are in the picture? When you start to count them, something strange happens. Instead of *looking down* on three blocks from the top, you find that you are *looking up* at five blocks from the bottom. No matter how hard you try, you cannot keep seeing the blocks the same way for more than a few seconds.

The second picture is made up of eight triangles. What do you see? First you may see something that looks like a red cross. Before you know it, you don't see a red cross anymore. You see a white cross instead. Then you see the red cross again. No matter how hard you try, you cannot keep the picture you see from changing.

The reason the pictures you see keep changing is because there are really two ways of seeing each picture. First you see each picture one way. After a while the brain gets tired from seeing the picture that way. Then it begins to see the picture the second way. When the brain gets tired from seeing the picture the second way, it begins to see it the first way once more.

Colors That Aren't There

There is a small red square at the top of this page.

Stare at the red square while you count slowly to thirty. Then move your eyes quickly so that you are staring at the black dot on the gray background. Soon you will see a bluish-green square on the gray background.

The bluish-green square isn't really there. It is an image that formed on your retina because you were staring at the red square. We call this kind of image an *after-image*. If you looked at an orange square, the after-image would be blue.

Your Eyes Can Sometimes Fool You

Look at the five pictures on the next page. Then answer these questions about the pictures.

Picture 1: Are the heavy black lines curved or are they straight? Are the top lines farther apart at the ends or in the middle? Are the bottom lines farther apart at the ends or in the middle?

Picture 2: This is a picture of a box. There are six stripes on the top of the box. Where are the stripes farthest apart? Which line is longer, a stripe or the side of the box marked h?

Picture 3: Which small square is larger, the small white square or the small black square?

Picture 4: Which line is longer, a or b?

Picture 5: Which arrow is longer, c or d?

Now use a ruler to see if your answers were correct. You have probably discovered that your eyes fooled you.

You have learned, from seeing them, that railroad tracks are straight. They go on and on and never meet. So when you look at straight railroad tracks that go on and on, you expect them to come together the way they do in Picture 5. You expect the stripes on the top of the box in Picture 2 to come together the way railroad tracks do. But the stripes do *not* come together. So they seem to separate.

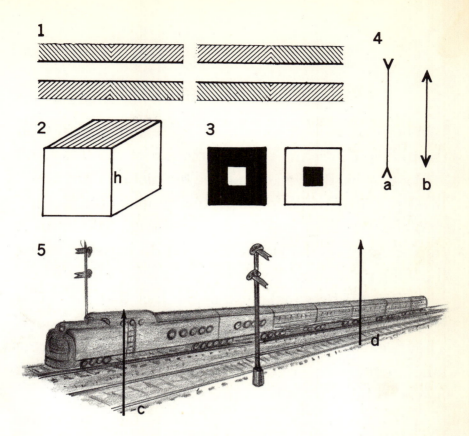

You have learned, from seeing them, that things look smaller when they are farther away. So arrow *d* should *look* smaller than arrow *c*, because it seems to be farther away. But it *isn't* smaller. So arrow *d* looks bigger than arrow *c*.

Light things always look larger than dark things. So the small white square in Picture 3 *looks* larger than the small black square even though they are the same size.

People say that seeing is believing. Now you know that sometimes it isn't.

Seeing Things That Aren't There

When you look at something, light from it shines on the retina. The retina makes a picture of the thing you are looking at. But you do not see the picture right away. It takes a little while for the retina to make the picture.

When you stop looking at something, light from it stops shining on the retina. But you do not stop seeing the thing right away. You keep seeing it for a little while.

Motion pictures make use of the fact that the retina works this way. Motion pictures do not really move. They are made by a special kind of camera. The camera takes pictures, one right after another, of the thing that moves. It takes 16 pictures in a second.

When the motion picture is shown, the pictures are flashed on a screen, one right after the other. The eye keeps seeing each picture even when the next picture is flashed on the screen. So all of the pictures seem to be joined together. Instead of seeing many separate pictures, you see one picture that seems to move.

The picture on your television screen does not move either. The strange way the retina acts is one of the reasons you see a moving picture on a television screen.

You can make your own movies by flipping the pages of this book. If you flip the pages and look at the eye in

the lower corner of each odd-numbered page, the eye
will wink. Of course, the eye is really not winking. Each
picture is a little different from the one before it. If you
flip the pages fast, the pictures seem to be joined. This
makes the eye seem to wink.

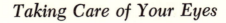

Taking Care of Your Eyes

To take good care of your eyes, be sure to have good lighting for the things you do close at hand.

When you read, your lamp should never be right in front of you. It is better for your eyes if there are other lights on, too. It is easier to read if the print is clear and not very small. It is easier to read, too, if the paper is not shiny.

You can help your eyes see things more clearly. If you are working with something light and shiny, work on a dark surface. If you are working with something dark, work on a light surface. Then the thing you are working with will be easier to see.

To protect your eyes, do not let bright light shine into them. Skiers know that snow makes the bright sunlight even brighter. Sunbathers know that water and white sand make the bright sunlight even brighter. They wear sunglasses to keep too much light out of their eyes.

If you take good care of your eyes, they will work for you as long as you live.

Word List

Albino (al-BY-no) — A person who has no coloring in his eyes, skin or hair.

Braille (BRAIL) — The raised letters used by blind people for reading with their fingertips.

Concave lens (KON-cave) — A lens that is thinner in the middle than it is at the edge.

Convex lens (KON-vex) — A lens that is thicker in the middle than it is at the edge.

Cornea (CORE-nee-a) — The clear cover over the front of the eyeball.

Focus (FOE-cuss) — To bend light, the way a lens does, to form a picture on a screen.

Fovea (FO-vee-a) — The spot on the retina where the clearest picture is formed.

Image (IMM-ij) — The picture formed by light that is bent by a lens.

Iris (EYE-riss) — The colored part of the eye.

Lens — The part of the eye that bends light to make a picture on the retina.

Optic nerve (OP-tick) — The bundle of fine threads that carry messages from the retina to the brain.

Pupil — The dark opening in the iris that lets light into the eye.

Retina (RET-in-a) — The part of the eye on which light shines.

Stereoscope (STEER-ee-o-scope) — A viewer for seeing a 3D picture made out of two flat pictures.

About the Authors

Irving and Ruth Adler have written more than three dozen books about science and mathematics. Dr. Adler has been an instructor in mathematics at Columbia University and at Bennington College, and was formerly head of the mathematics department of a New York City high school. Mrs. Adler, who formerly taught mathematics, science, and art in schools in the New York area, recently also taught in Bennington. In addition to working with her husband writing this book, she drew the illustrations.

Books by Irving Adler alone and books by him in collaboration with Ruth Adler have been printed in 55 different foreign editions, in 8 languages and in 9 paperback editions.

The Adlers now live in the country in Shaftsbury Township, near Bennington, Vermont.

PHOTOGRAPH CREDITS

Page 5 — Eye test chart — American Optical Co.
Page 23 — Irving Adler
Page 27 — Bausch and Lomb
Page 31 — American Foundation for the Blind
Page 34 — The Seeing Eye, Morristown, N.J.
Page 44 — Movie film — Eastman Kodak Co.

ACC-79

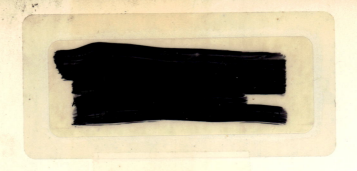